Unit 2

HOUGHTON MIFFLIN HARCOURT
School Publishers

Photo credits

Cover © GORDON & CATHY ILLG/Animals Animals - Earth Scenes. **Title** John Foxx/Stockbyte/Getty Images. **9** © Juniors Bildarchiv/Alamy. **10** © imagebroker/Alamy. **11** © Ron Niebrugge/Alamy. **12** Comstock. **13** © Don Geyer/Alamy. **14** © Juniors Bildarchiv/Alamy. **15** John Foxx/Stockbyte/Getty Images. **16** © ImageState/Alamy. **33** Ralph Lee Hopkins/National Geographic/Getty Images. **34** © Visual&Written SL/Alamy. **35** © Tim Keatley/Alamy. **36** © Jupiterimages/Creatas/Alamy. **37** © PhotoDisc/Alamy. **38** © DLILLC/Corbis. **39** © Albaimages/Alamy. **40** © Neal and Molly Jansen/Alamy.

Copyright © 2014 by Houghton Mifflin Harcourt Publishing Company

Printed in the U.S.A.

ISBN-13: 978-0-547-86698-7

14 0868   21 20 19 18 17 16 15
4500525421   A B C D E F G

Contents

A Job for Bob

by Harry Tolan
illustrated by Diane Blasius

This is Bob Bear. Bob has a job.
Animals like Bob. Bob is a big help.
His job is a big help to them. Bob can
bring them gifts.

At his work, Bob got this big tan box. This box had no name on its tag, but Bob must take it to the right animal.

2

Was this box sent for Frank Fox?
Bob went to his stump. Bob rang.
Ding dong! Ding dong! Ding dong!

3

Frank Fox was at home. Frank did not
take the box that Bob had. It was not his
box. Bob left Frank Fox. Bob went on.

Was this box sent for Bev Bat?

Next, Bob went to her cave. Bob rang.

Ding dong! Ding dong! Ding dong!

Bev Bat was at home. Bev did not take
the box that Bob had. It was not for Bev.
Bob left Bev Bat and Bob went on.

Was this box sent for Sal Snake?
Next, Bob went to his lake. Bob rang.
Ding dong! Ding dong! Ding dong!

Sal Snake did take that big, tan box!
It was his gift. "Thanks, Bob! Thanks!"
said Sal. "Good work, Bob!"

This is a baby skunk. It is a skunk kit.
[Thi]s skunk kit is on this big log. This
[sku]nk kit can jump up on this log.

Baby Animals

by Kate Pistone

What can baby animals do?

9

This is a baby fox. It is a fox pup.
This fox pup is in its den. This fox pup
can nap in its den, but it can get up in
a wink. This fox pup is up.

This baby is in its nes[
mom. Mom and her baby
Mom can flap her wings,
can not flap yet. Not yet.

Thi
sku

This baby is a kid. This kid is with its
mom. Mom and her kid are next to this
lake. Mom and her kid can get a drink.

This is a baby bear. It is a bear cub.
This cub is at a big pond. This cub can
get a fish. It is work to get fish, but this
cub must eat.

This baby is on the sand. It is a pup.
Mom and her pup can swim. Then, they
can rest in the sand. This pup can get as
big as her mom.

This baby is soft. It is a baby rabbit.
It can eat plants. It can hop and hop and
hop! It can run, too.

Jill and Mack

by Sara Nicholas
illustrated by Rick Powell

Jill and Mack met their duck pals in the spring grass.

"Stand up and smile," said Jill.

With a click, click, click, Jill got five pretty pictures.

"It is game time," said Mack.

Mack swung his leg to kick. The grass
was wet and slick. Mack fell on his back.

"Do not fuss," said Mack as he got up.
"I am just fine."

Riff will kick next. Riff swung his leg
to kick. Riff is quick, but Riff did not kick
the ball. Riff sat and Jill came to kick.
Can Jill kick it?

Jill had strong legs. Jill swung her leg
to kick. With a swift kick, the ball went
up, up, up in the air. Jill ran and ran.

20

Mack went to block the fast ball, but it
went up, up, up and past Mack. Mack ran
and ran. Can Mack get it?

Jill saw the clock. Tick, tock. Where is Mack? Tick, tock. What if Mack fell? Tick, tock. What if Mack is stuck?

22

Jill led the ducks to Mack.

"Do not fuss," said Mack. "I am a duck. I had a nice quick dip."

Jill and the ducks dive in and swim.
"Is it still game time?" said Mack.
"Yes. It is still game time," said Jill.
Jill and the ducks went back.

Rabbit's Muffins

by Cynthia Rothman
illustrated by Tim Egan

In tennis class, Rabbit swung at the
tennis ball and hit it up, up, up. Rabbit
had made her best and last hit. Rabbit
was late and went home.

Rabbit has a job. Rabbit must make
muffins. Rabbit will blend milk, eggs,
and muffin mix. Rabbit will fill pans and
pop the pans in to bake.

Rabbit will ride and bring muffins to Cow and Pig. Rabbit did not stop at the home of Puffin. Rabbit just rode past his home. Rabbit had no muffin for him.

Puffin got on his bike. He rode his
bike to see Rabbit.

"You gave Cow and Pig muffins.
Why did Cow and Pig get muffins, but I
did not?" said Puffin.

"I did not think puffins like muffins,"
said Rabbit. "Puffins dive and swim for
puffin food."

"Yes," said Puffin, "puffins do, but
puffins can like muffins, too."

"Sorry," said Rabbit. "Next time, you will get muffins."

"Thanks," said Puffin, and rode his bike back home.

Rabbit got pretty pictures. Rabbit made muffins with the same shapes.

Rabbit made stacks of muffins. Puffin and his puffin pals like the muffins that Rabbit made. Those muffins are such a big hit. Rabbit will bake muffins for puffins, and cows and pigs, as fast as she can. Rabbit will bake a lot.

Still today, Puffin and his puffin pals get in line for muffins as muffin smells fill the air. Muffins made by Rabbit are still a big, big hit.

Splish! Splash! Whales

by Sara Spring

Splish! Splash! Splish!

Whales live in water like fish. Whales swim like fish, but whales are not fish.

Fish take in air while they swim. Whales can not. Whales must swim up to get air.

Splish! Splash! Splish!

Blue whales are huge. In fact, no other animal on land or in water can be as big as these whales.

These whales have strong fins. Fins help whales swim fast.

Splish! Splash! Splish!

White whales are not as big as most whales. The skin on this whale is as white as milk.

White whales swim in water that is very cold. White whales dive and hunt.

Splish! Splash! Splish!

Dolphins are whales, not fish. This dolphin must swim up to get air. That hole on its head lets air in and lets it out.

Dolphins have strong fins. Fins help dolphins swim.

Splish! Splash! Splish!
Dolphins swim with each other
in pods. Dolphin pods can be a few
dolphins or many dolphins. Dolphins
make clicks and squeaks that help them
set a safe path in the water.

Splish! Splash! Splish!
Dolphins play games with other
dolphins. Dolphins chase each other.
Dolphins jump and dive and play.

Splish! Splash! Splish!
Dolphins catch waves and ride them.
Dolphins spring up and dive. Dolphins
are strong and can jump high.

People think dolphins are wise.
Dolphins can hear well and see well.

Trish is on this ship. Trish has her
eyes on those dolphins. She will watch
them and take pictures.

Smile, dolphins! Smile at Trish!

Drifting Up, Up, Up

by Emily Banks
illustrated by Teri Sloat

Scamp makes a kite with white paper and sticks. Scamp adds a long, long red string. Scamp likes his white kite with its red string.

"Quite a nice kite!" thinks Scamp.

Scamp rushed to look out. It was wet,
wet, wet. Scamp wished he could fly his
kite, but he could not.

Scamp kept his eyes on his kite as he
munched on nut crunch.

Scamp got up. He saw that it was
not wet, and that leaves swished. Scamp
dashed out and felt the wind on his back.

"It is time to fly this kite," yelled
Scamp. "It's time! It's time!"

Scamp ran fast, huffing and puffing,
with his kite until the wind lifted it up.

His kite was drifting, when a strong
wind gust came. His kite swished and
landed on a branch.

With a few tugs, Bird got his kite and
gave it to Scamp.

"Fly this kite at a field," hinted Bird.
"That is the best place."

"Thanks," yelled Scamp as he went on.

Scamp ran fast, huffing and puffing,
with his kite until the wind lifted it up.
As it drifted, a strong gust of wind came.
His kite swished. Scamp lost his grip on
the kite string. The kite string landed in
a pond. Frog was jumping there.

Frog swam to get the string, splashing as he went. Frog handed it to Scamp.

"Grasp the string and hold on," hinted Frog. "Grasp it."

"Thanks," said Scamp, clutching his kite string. "Nice hint."

Scamp ran fast, huffing and puffing, with his kite. The wind lifted his white kite and it drifted up, up, up.

"People will think I am good at this," Scamp thought, "and, I am!"

Maybe So

by Vincent Paulsen
illustrated by Meryl Treatner

"Is it time yet?" asked Mel. "Can we go soon? Can we?"

Mel kept asking until his mom asked him to please stop asking.

"I am afraid we must just sit a while, Mel. Dad is still at his job. He must finish his work. Until Dad is finished, we can not go," said Mom.

"Well, can we make up a game?" asked Mel. "Let's make up a letter game."

Mom and Mel made up "Spell It."
Mel is a spelling champ. He likes spelling
games. Mom is pretty good at spelling,
too. Today in this game, Mel even spelled
"wood" and "would." Then, at last, Dad
came. "We can go!" yelled Mel.

Mel picked up his bag. Dad picked up the rest. Mom got the fins and stuff. Mom went out last and locked up.

Mel began thinking and thinking about this trip. What will it be like?

Mel kept thinking as he got on the jet. Would he swim with dolphins? Would dolphins let him swim with their pod? Would a nice big dolphin jump with Mel riding on his back? Maybe. Maybe not.

Mel kept thinking while he was flying in the jet. Would he visit with puffins? Maybe he would dive with them and look at red and yellow fish. He would swim deep, like a puffin.

Then maybe he would swim up with them. He would rest on his raft. Mel would rest and rock on big waves. He would rise up with each wave and then slide back down with the puffins.

Mel kept thinking as the jet landed.
Maybe, if a nice white whale swam
next to Mel, it would take him on a fast
white whale ride. Maybe! Maybe not.
What do you think Mel will do?

Racing Away!

by Cynthia Rothman
illustrated by Tim Bowers

The sun was rising as Snake, Duck,
Bear, and Frog were waking up.

Clang! Clang! Clang!

Clang! Clang! Clang!

Who kept on ringing that bell?

It was Fox. He waved his hands and
asked Snake, Duck, Bear, and Frog to sit.

Fox had a big note. It said, "Come and
be in this great race."

"Which race will it be?" asked Snake.

"We must have a race that most of us
want," said Fox.

"We must vote, then," said Bear.

Snake is hoping it will be a sliding race. Snake is good at sliding.

Duck is hoping it will be a gliding race. Duck is good at gliding.

Bear is hoping it will be a hiking race. Bear is good at hiking.

Frog is hoping it will be a jumping race. Frog is good at jumping.

Fox named a race and Snake, Duck,
Bear, and Frog voted. Snake voted for
sliding. Duck voted for a gliding race.
Bear voted for hiking. Frog voted for
jumping. Every race got one vote.

Voting did not help them much.

"Can we have an ice skating race?" asked Fox. "No one is good at that."

"Yes. We all would have an even chance in that race," added Snake.

Fox went on the ice first, but landed on his back. Then Fox got up and skated.
Bear slid and fell and slid and fell. Then Bear skated with grace. Snake traced an "S" with his skate.

Frog got up and skated. Frog spun and spun on the ice. Duck was afraid, but soon he skated and went fast.

Fox, Snake, Bear, Duck, and Frog just skated and smiled. Skating was fun.

"This is the best race," yelled Frog.

"Yes," said Bear. "Next time we can have a baking race. No one is good at baking things."

"That would be fun!" added Fox. "We can bake and snack."

Let's Have Fun

by Kate Pistone
illustrated by Diana Schoenbrun

Will Whale woke up in his huge home.
Sunshine danced on his face as he rolled
out of bed. He swam to his table and had
his kelp and eggs.

"I think I want to swim and splash.
I'll find Steve Squid and we'll have fun,"
said Will. Will went to visit Steve Squid.
Will gave Steve a tug and smiled.

"Let's go for a swim," said Will.

"I'm afraid I can't," said Steve. "See my trumpet? I can't jump and swim and splash today. Ask me next time."

Next, Will went to visit Cam Clam in the sand. Will gave her shell a tap and smiled. Can Cam swim and splash?

"Let's ride those waves," said Will.

"I would really like to," said Cam, "but I'm baking a cake. Ask me next time."

Then, Will went to the cove because he wanted to visit Frank Fish. Will gave his fin a pat and smiled. "Let's splish and splash," said Will to Frank.

"Fine!" said Frank. "I'll go with you!
That will be fun!" So Will and Frank
went here and there. They smiled and
joked all day long.

Then, Steve and Cam came to splish and splash, too. Will and Frank and Steve and Cam swam a while, and then Cam gave them cake. "That's what I call a whale of a time!" said Will.

I'm Going to Win

by Kiyoshi Fukuhara
illustrated by Bob Monahan

It is race day at the pond! Animals
came from all around to see the big
contest. "I will run and win! I will run,
run, run so fast!" Croc said.

First, they had to run on sand. Stripes,
Croc, and Deb lined up. Frog yelled
"Dash!" and dash they did.

It's hot on that sand, but they do not
mind that hot sand.

Croc, Stripes, and Deb ran on.

Deb ran past Croc. "Deb is fast! She's fast! Really fast! I'm drifting behind! I've got to glide, glide, glide to the finish line," said Croc.

Next, they had to swim in the pond.
Stripes, Croc, and Deb jumped in. It's
really cold in that pond, but they do not
mind that cold pond.

Word Lists

A Job for Bob

page 1

Decodable Words
Target Skill: *Common Final Clusters nd, ng, nk, nt, ft, xt, mp*
bring, ding, dong, Frank, gift, gifts, left, next, rang, sent, Snake, stump, thanks, went

Words Using Previously Taught Skills
at, Bat, Bev, big, Bob, box, but, can, cave, did, Fox, got, had, has, help, his, home, is, it, its, job, lake, like, must, name, no, not, on, Sal, tag, take, tan, that, them, this

High-Frequency Words
New
animals, bear, work

Previously Taught
a, animal, for, good, her, right, said, the, to, was

Baby Animals

page 9

Decodable Words
Target Skill: *Common Final Clusters nd, ng, nk, nt, ft, xt, mp*
and, drink, jump, pond, sand, skunk, soft, wings, wink

Words Using Previously Taught Skills
as, at, baby, big, but, can, cub, den, fish, flap, fox, get, hop, in, is, it, its, kid, kit, lake, like, log, mom, must, nap, nest, not, on, plants, pup, rabbit, rest, run, swim, then, this, up, yet

High-Frequency Words
New
animals, bear, work

Previously Taught
a, are, do, eat, her, they, too, what, with

Jill and Mack

page 17

Decodable Words
Target Skill: *Double consonants and ck*
back, block, click, clock, duck, ducks,
fell, fuss, grass, Jill, kick, Mack, quick,
Riff, slick, still, stuck, tick, tock, will

Words Using Previously Taught Skills
am, and, as, but, came, can, did, dip,
dive, fast, fine, five, game, get, got,
had, he, his, in, is, it, just, led, leg, legs,
met, next, nice, not, on, pals, past, ran,
sat, smile, spring, stand, strong, swift,
swim, swung, time, up, went, wet, yes

High-Frequency Words
New
air, pictures, pretty

Previously Taught
a, ball, do, I, said, saw, the,
their, to, was, where, with

Rabbit's Muffins

page 25

Decodable Words
Target Skill: *VCCV Pattern (with double consonants)*
muffin, muffins, puffin, puffins,
rabbit, tennis

Target Skill: *Double consonants and ck*
back, class, fill, smells, stacks, still

Words Using Previously Taught Skills
and, as, at, bake, best, big, bike, blend,
bring, but, can, Cow, did, dive, eggs,
fast, gave, get, got, had, has, him, his,
hit, home, in, job, just, last, late, like,
line, lot, made, make, milk, mix, must,
next, not, on, pals, pans, past, Pig,
pop, ride, rode, same, shapes, she,
stop, such, swim, swung, time, up,
went, will, yes

High-Frequency Words
New
air, pictures, pretty

Previously Taught
a, are, ball, by, do, food, for,
her, I, no, of, said, see, sorry,
the, think, those, to, today,
too, was, why, with, you

Splish! Splash! Whales!

page 33

Decodable Words
Target Skill: *Consonant digraphs th, sh, wh, ch, tch, ph*
catch, chase, dolphins, fish, path, ship, splash, splish, that, them, these, think, this, those, whale, whales, while, white

Words Using Previously Taught Skills
as, at, big, but, can, clicks, die, dive, each, fact, fast, fins, games, get, has, help, hole, huge, hunt, in, its, jump, land, lets, like, live, make, milk, must, not, on, pods, ride, safe, set, skin, smile, spring, strong, swim, take, Trish, up, well, wise, with

High-Frequency Words
New
eyes, few, people

Previously Taught
a, air, animal, are, be, blue, cold, have, head, hear, her, high, many, most, or, other, out, pictures, play, see, she, the, they, to, very, watch, water

Drifting Up, Up, Up

Decodable Words
Target Skill: *Base words and endings -s, -ed, -ing*
clutching, dashed, drifted, drifting, handed, hinted, huffing, jumping, landed, lifted, likes, makes, munched, puffing, rushed, splashing, sticks, swished, thanks, thinks, tugs, wished, yelled

Target Skill: *Consonant digraphs th, sh, wh, ch, tch, ph*
branch, clutching, crunch, dashed, munched, rushed, splashing, swished, thanks, that, think, thinks, this, when, white, wished

Words Using Previously Taught Skills
adds, am, an, and, as, at, back, best, but, came, fast, felt, Frog, gave, get, got, grasp, grip, gust, hint, his, it, it's, its, kept, kite, long, lost, nice, not, nut, on, place, pond, quite, ran, red, Scamp, string, strong, swam, time, until, up, went, wet, will, wind, with

High-Frequency Words
New
eyes, few, people

Previously Taught
a, bird, could, field, fly, good, he, hold, I, look, out, paper, saw, there, thought, to, was

Maybe So

page 49

Decodable Words
Target Skill: *Base words and endings -ed, -ing (including spelling change of drop final e)*

asked, asking, finished, flying, landed, locked, picked, riding, spelled, spelling, thinking, yelled

Words Using Previously Taught Skills
am, and, as, at, back, bag, big, can, champ, Dad, deep, dive, dolphin, dolphins, each, fast, finish, fins, fish, game, got, him, his, in, is, it, jet, job, jump, just, kept, last, let, let's, letter, like, likes, made, make, Mel, mom, must, next, nice, not, on, pod, puffin, puffins, raft, red, rest, rid, rise, rock, sit, slide, Spell, still, stop, stuff, swam, swim, take, them, then, think, this, time, trip, until, up, visit, waves, well, went, whale, while, white, will, with, yet

High-Frequency Words
New
afraid, kept, would

Previously Taught
a, about, be, began, do, down, even, go, good, he, I, look, maybe, out, please, pretty, said, soon, the, their, to, today, too, was, we, what, work, yellow, you

Racing Away!

page 57

Decodable Words

Target Skill: *VCV pattern*
baking, gliding, hiking, hoping, rising, skated, skating, sliding, voted, voting, waking

Target Skill: *Base words and endings -ed, -ing (including spelling change of drop final e)*
added, asked, jumping, landed, named, ringing, smiled, traced, waved, yelled

Words Using Previously Taught Skills
an, and, as, at, back, bake, bell, best, big, but, can, chance, clang, did, Duck, fast, fell, Fox, Frog, fun, got, grace, had, hands, help, his, ice, in, is, it, just, much, must, next, not, note, on, race, sit, slid, snack, Snake, spun, sun, that, them, then, things, this, time, up, us, vote, want, went, which, will, with, yes

High-Frequency Words

New
afraid, kept, would

Previously Taught
a, all, be, bear, come, even, every, first, for, good, great, have, he, most, no, of, one, said, soon, the, to, was, we, were, who

Let's Have Fun

page 65

Decodable Words
Target Skill: *Contractions*
can't, I'll, I'm, let's, that's, we'll

Words Using Previously Taught Skills
and, as, ask, baking, bed, but, cake, call, Cam, came, can, Clam, cove, danced, eggs, face, fin, fine, Fish, Frank, fun, gave, had, his, home, huge, in, joked, jump, kelp, like, long, me, next, on, pat, ride, rolled, sand, shell, smiled, splash, splish, Squid, Steve, sunshine, swam, swim, tap, that, them, then, think, those, time, trumpet, tug, up, visit, want, wanted, waves, went, whale, while, will, Will, woke

High-Frequency Words
New
because, really, you

Previously Taught
a, afraid, all, be, find, for, go, have, he, her, here, I, my, of, out, said, see, table, the, there, to, they, today, too, what, would

I'm Going to Win

page 73

Decodable Words

Target Skill: *Contractions*
can't, he's, I'm, I've, it's, she's

Words Using Previously Taught Skills

and, at, away, big, bike, broke, but, came, contest, Croc, dash, Deb, did, drifting, fast, finish, Frog, glide, got, had, held, helped, his, hot, in, is, it, jumped, like, line, lined, long, mind, next, not, on, past, path, pond, prize, pumped, race, ran, ride, rode, run, sand, splash, Stripes, swam, swim, thanks, that, up, will, win, wind, yelled

High-Frequency Words

New
because, really, you

Previously Taught

all, animals, around, be, behind, cold, do, fall, first, give, go, me, said, see, the, they, to